Introduction

About Us

We have been in "the Lifestyle" for a combined total of over a decade. That might not seem like a great deal of time but it's amazing what you can learn when you have a willing partner who is enthusiastic and caring.

Neither of us started out in the roles we are in now. It took us both some time to realize who and what we are. If you are confused, it may help you to take three quizzes. The first is the BDSM Role quiz which can be found online. The second is any Myer-Briggs Personality Test. The third is The Love Languages quiz.

I started out as a Master/Dominant and she started as a submissive. Our roles fluctuate a lot. However we are primarily Daddy Dom and babygirl and as such, the purpose of this book is to help burgeoning Daddies and littles have some guidance for a better experience as they take this journey.

In addition to our writings we asked for contributions from Fetlife users and wherever they contributed we noted their Fetlife username.

Assumptions and Warnings

We make some assumptions in this book.

The first assumption is that you have at least a reasonable and passing familiarity with BDSM and "the Lifestyle". If you do not, there are a number of great books out there that will introduce you properly. Jay Wiseman's excellent SM 101 is a good starter. As is Screw The Roses, Send Me The Thorns by Phillip Miller.

The second assumption is that you know how to play safely. That you know about negotiation and consent and safewords. Though we talk about some of these things here, we DO NOT cover them in depth. This book is for informational purposes only, and as such, we are not responsible for any physical or mental harm resulting from your acting upon this information with or without additional guidance from other resources.

The third assumption is less an assumption and more of a statement. Everything written in this book is from our perspective. And as such it's written in a form that is gender and orientation specific to us. So when I say Daddy, if you are a Mommy you can just change it in your head. I did this to be succinct rather than to be offensive.

The fourth assumption is that you know of our favorite kink site: Fetlife.com. We mention it a few times in this book. Fetlife is where my babygirl and I met and played a big influence on this book as most of the writings originated there from us or others.

The fifth assumption is that you have at least a scholarly desire to learn about the DD/lg dynamic. Otherwise you would not be reading this. So enjoy!

What Is DD/lg?

DD/lg FAQ

Note: DD/lg is the gender/name dynamic I chose because it's ours. Any gender or orientation works in this dynamic.

What is DD/lg?

DD/lg stands for Daddy Dominant/little girl. Basically, the Dominant is more of a nurturing caretaker than a strict disciplinarian like in a Master/slave or regular D/s relationship. The little side is "young acting" and usually the little side stays tucked away until it's safe to come out. Some likes and personalities are always there and some (young speak, for example) may be hidden until private times.

So a DD is a weaker Dominant?

I don't think so. All labels come with certain expectations. Daddy Dominants have all the same characteristics as regular Dominants, but in my opinion they have to possess more patience and have to have the ability to be a little silly.

So a little is a person with multiple personalities?

No. A little just finds joy and pleasure in a dynamic in which they can shed their adult "skin" for a bit and be spoiled and taken care of.

Do people have sex this way?

Yes. Though for us the sex is usually more D/s and S/M than anything else. Some young speak occurs.

She may dress up in little clothing. She calls me Daddy. She asks for permission for things.

Doesn't that make you a pedophile?

NO. There's no part of us that doesn't understand we are two consenting adults having sex and a relationship. It's like calling a sadist an abusive asshole because they hit people. Daddy Dominants aren't attracted to children in the least.

So a little can't function in the real world?

Chances are there are doctors and lawyers and politicians who are little. We've seen a public figure or famous actress on TV and more than once came to the conclusion that they have little tendencies. My babygirl is an EMT and was working as one when we met. She saved lives and never reverted to a younger age in the middle just like a sadist wouldn't start beating people out of the blue.

What are the major differences between a DD/lg and a D/s dynamic?

In many ways the lines are quite blurry. Our dynamic is a DD/lg, D/s, and S/M dynamic with primal tendencies. Littles are just submissives with tendencies to act younger and do younger things. Daddies are Dominants who are a little more nurturing and strict, but in a fatherly manner. DD's tend to use lines as punishment (but not always). We reward with candy or stuffies. Littles like to feel owned just like other submissives but they need to feel safe in higher ways.

What is a stuffie?

A stuffed animal. Littles collect these like crack fiends collect rocks.

What are lines?

Lines are a form of punishment not limited to the DD/lg dynamic but occur more commonly there. Lines are a repeated sentence written over and over again by disobedient littles. The repeated sentence should be in the form of a lesson or oath such as, "I will not put glitter in Daddy's underwear".

I don't like candy or cartoons or stuffies. Can I be a little?

Personally I hate labels, but I also hate misrepresentation. If you have little tendencies you should state this to any potential mates. Tendencies might be as limited as calling someone "Daddy" during sex. But there is no limit on calling yourself a little. Just be aware that a partner might view that differently than you do.

I don't like candy or cartoons or stuffies. Can I be a Daddy?

Again, I'm not a fan of labels or misrepresentation. This is where patience comes in. You don't have to like these things, but you have to be ok with being with someone who does. If you are unable to tolerate these things or a person who reverts to a state where they do silly and playful things you should probably move on (for everyone's peace of mind).

I'm a (insert gender) of (insert orientation) and I like to be called and treated like and called (Daddy/Mommy/Genderless Pronoun Big Person). Is this ok?

Do whatever makes you and your partner happy. Everyone has to find out what they are and what they need. As long as that's the goal, then go crazy.

Being a Daddy

Introduction

As with any BDSM dynamic, being a Daddy is a complicated thing. There are many intricacies to being a good Daddy Dom. I'm a Daddy Dom with many many different sides.

Some people may not understand how your sides fit together but I hope in this chapter to kind of illustrate how I fit many roles within this one. For the Daddy Dom reading, you must find your parts that fit you and incorporate them how you see fit.

Qualities of A Daddy Dominant

For me, I've identified several key qualities which I feel make me a Daddy Dom. These are good qualities for ANY Dominant role but to me these make the most sense for Daddies.

Qualities:

Honesty
Trustworthiness
Patience
Leadership
Compassion
Commitment
Observant

Honesty

Nothing says lack of Dominance as much as not enough courage to speak honestly and in a manner that is forthright. Nothing says I can't be in control of you as showing I can't be in control of me either.

This is not just being honest with your partner; your babygirl and submissive. No, its also about being honest with yourself. What do you want? What are your hopes and fears and dreams? If you can't be honest with yourself about this, you are leading two people down a path of ruin.

Trustworthiness

A Daddy must trust his submissive and must trust in that submission. That trust cannot be blind trust. That trust also requires verification. As Henry Ford is supposed to have said: Trust, but verify.

Patience

I think the other qualities are probably pretty obvious. But patience might be the most often overlooked quality, in my opinion. It's kind of an ongoing joke between Dominants that we want what we want and we want it right now. At least I hope that's a joke. A Daddy should be deliberate and take their time with a babygirl.

We have to learn who they are and know what makes them tick before we can do the things. I think this is key, rather than just jumping in and applying a broad brush to the act itself.

Leadership

This is pretty self-explanatory. You have to be able to make decisions, plans and lead. That's the very basic of the D side of the slash.

Compassion

This is another often overlooked quality. You don't need to be a so-called sensual Dominant to need compassion. Compassion doesn't entail a sense of weakness, but rather the ability to know what others are feeling. So maybe empathy is a better word. But a Daddy has to be able to understand his actions and the reactions of the babygirl.

Commitment

A Daddy must be committed, and not only in the relationship with the babygirl. They must be committed to learning and improving themselves. They must be committed to growing the relationship and dynamic with a babygirl.

Observant

Being observant is a good quality for a Daddy to have, for several reasons. The first is obvious. A lot of information is all gathered through observing and knowing the submissive in the context of a scene.

A really great Daddy also observes a babygirl outside of those places. The Daddy knows when the babygirl is uncomfortable or sad or scared in just plain daily life. Some people consider it a badge of honor to make their submissive uncomfortable. I say, to each their own. I like to create an environment where the babygirl feels like they can be themselves. I think that comes through observing, watching for times when they aren't acting themselves.

Those are the qualities I think of when I consider how to be a better Dominant. Those are the qualities I feel are important. Which are important to you?

So You Want To Be A Daddy?

You are perusing Fetlife one day and you happen upon a picture of a cute girl. And she's close! And she's single! little? babygirl? Oh, this chick likes to dress up in little girl clothes and school girl outfits and pretend your cock is one big pacifier that she can go to sleep sucking! Awesome dude.

So you let her call you Daddy. Because that's hot, right? And the sex is great and the age regression is cute and hot and she's eager to please. But what's all this shit about cuddling and watching cartoons? - you hate cartoons. And the cute things she did are suddenly annoying and the next shiny thing comes along and off you go.

Calling yourself a Daddy is not the same as calling yourself a Dominant and ordering someone around. It's not the same as calling yourself a sadist and swinging a paddle or flogger. You can fake that shit. You cannot fake being a Daddy. You can swing the paddle and that takes no skill and you don't even have to be into it. You can't go through the Daddy motions and hope it works out.

Deceiving and abandoning any person is a heinous thing. When you deceive a little you are abandoning a person but you are killing that little. Some will suppress the little as long as they can. Ultimately the little always pops back out. But after a string of abandonments the little will go into hiding a little longer each time. And it's like taking something beautiful and breaking it.

Being a Daddy is a commitment. It's waking up at 3am with the thunder because your little gets scared. It's watching the same cartoon for the 800th time because it makes your little happy. It's spending the extra money for candy at the movies. It's about never finishing a conversation because they get distracted. It's about making something about more than sex and yourself for once.

So if you want to be with a person who identifies as little, be honest with them. They know how to protect their little. But deceiving them into revealing this side of them for your own gains when you don't plan on nurturing it is just shitty and wrong.

Part Time Daddy

I can't be a part time Daddy.

When you wake up to the roar of thunder crashing down as it rattles the house and wake me to be comforted. I won't be bothered in the least.

But when I tell you that you can't do something that might hurt you. You have to understand where I'm coming from.

When you want to watch cartoons and color I may act annoyed. But its just an act and I'm just teasing. I'll watch them with you.

But when I need you to fall to your knees I hope you realize I desire my submissive little.

When you need to be fucked like my babygirl and told you are a good girl and made to feel good you will get that.

But sometimes I just need you to be my little fucktoy and take it for Daddy.

I'll cuddle you and pet your head and give you a bath.

And then I'll beat you until you are bruised and crying.

And then I'll cuddle you some more.

I'll do these things because I care about you; because you are my property and I own you and also because I love you.

Just don't ask me to be Daddy some of the time.

Because I need my babygirl all of the time.

The Love of a Daddy

The love of a Daddy is such a special beautiful love. One that wraps his babygirl up in a warm blanket like a never ending hug. A Daddy's love is strong enough to put all the pieces back together again no matter how broken she feels inside.

The love of a Daddy brightens up the darkest of days. He knows just which stuffy will save the day, and exactly where they are at all times. He knows what Disney movie will make his baby feel better when she's sick. He cuddles her and makes all her favorite silly faces until she giggles.

The love of a Daddy is patient and accepting, and fills a babygirl's heart confidence. He knows she will make mistakes, and that He will be right there to guide her through it. Sometimes He will feel like He is being "the bad guy", but we know it's because He loves us and wants to keep us safe.

The love of a Daddy has filled my life with such purpose. He has given me so much love and support that I've grown into a stronger woman than I would have ever thought possible. With my Daddy's love all things are possible and for Him I'm truly thankful.

Let Your little Be little

My babygirl's niece just reclaimed a coloring book and crayons that had been so rudely borrowed. The picture that my little colored was a multicolored kitty which was outstanding.

Of course I stood there impotently and watched this happen. I heard her say, "guess I can't be little today".

That broke my heart. We travelled 800 miles the past few days and I only wanted her to be able to find her little. She doesn't like flying and her mom beats her up on occasion.

I got a little frustrated. Then I realized that this is a situation a Daddy Dom can fix. So I picked up my iPad and opened a color by number app that I downloaded.

I think things like these are important. There are a million things that can pull a little out of little space. And a select few that can drag them in. And when one of those things pulls them out I feel it's the Daddy's responsibility to see if they can bring the little back.

You can't gripe about missing a little if you don't do things to help facilitate a space that shows them it's ok to be little. You have to find ways to let your little be little.

It's not always easy. It's not always without sacrifice. But if you are a Daddy Dom who enjoys your little, you'll make it happen.

Humble Dominant

It sometimes seems like "the Lifestyle" is really no place for a humble Dominant.

There is a certain, often unsaid, expectation that Dominants must constantly be a paragon of confidence and cool swagger. WE are the ones in control when the dynamic is set. We make the decisions. We steer the ship. We protect our s-types.

But we are fallible. We make mistakes. We worry. We sometimes even lose our confidence. I really wish that for a lot of people that didn't seem like something that's less than sexy.

I'm sure there are some who would argue that a Dominant with humility won't exhibit the strength and confidence needed to draw out their submission; to earn it. However, I feel like that's a recipe for disaster. Submission should never be something that has to be drawn out like blood from a vein. I'll show my honesty, my character and that I'm safe and fun. If that's not enough to spark the light of submission, then that flame just isn't meant to burn.

I always feel like I have things to learn. I'll always try to learn them. I have no problem admitting to another Dominant that they have more skills than me or do something better. I learn from new people and seasoned vets alike. Sometime I learn something when teaching others. There are a lot of us out there. We don't demand submission. We gain it by being ourselves.

Humble Dominants may not hit you as hard as you wish. But they also won't abuse your limits.

We will ask you too many times if you are alright. We might stop at "ouch" or "no" or a grimace on your face. This may seem unsexy, but it's because we care about you and don't want to hurt you in a way you don't want.

If you fight us, we may just give up because we don't feel you find us worthy of our submission. There are Dominants who will fight you back, but sometimes that's because they see you as something to win and not as a person (that's my opinion).

I think in the end we need to remember that those on both sides of the slash are people, and people aren't perfect. You can't expect your Dominant or submissive to be if you can't live up to that perfect ideal either.

Acts of Dominance

I know that heading will immediately raise ire. However, one should read "act" as a noun and not a verb. Anyone acting dominant without possessing that trait is usually found out pretty quick. But one can also be Dominant but not know how to show that properly.

I'm going back to BDSM 101 for a minute here. And I've been asked this question and always with a new Dominant coming onto the scene there's the confusion about exactly what to do. And usually we get the whiplash of overcompensating due to lack of knowledge and experience or being underwhelming for the same reasons. I had trouble with this at the first. Its especially difficult when you've been in a long relationship and you have to relearn all your behaviors as this side of you emerges.

Now I know there are tons of people who were born Dominant. Those of you who came out of the womb and smacked the doctor on the ass. But a lot of us pushed this side down because of what society thought and because of our upbringing or religion or what have you.

There are three realms of Dominance and different behaviors reign in each: In public, in private and in the bedroom. You and your partner may choose NOT to have a 24/7 relationship. You may choose to just have a dynamic in the bedroom. That's a personal decision and may affect your behaviors outside the bedroom or not. So take everything with a grain of salt.

In public is where a lot of us have to be more subtle and discreet. Again, I know there's someone out there that tells me they lead their sub around on a collar and leash in public but for most of us that's simply not an option. Speaking of collars - a day collar is a great discrete way to show ownership. Most people don't really notice it. Those who do usually say "nice necklace".

When it comes to leashes I prefer the leash that's felt and not seen. There are lots of ways to show this in public without being overt. And every dynamic is different so its a good idea to have the discussion with your submissive as part of negotiations. You don't want to offend them in public and something you think is ok might not be.

Some ways I like to let her know she's owned discretely in public.

Placing my hands somewhere that shows that. Now this doesn't mean groping. A hand placed on the lower back as you usher her through doors serves a good purpose. On a shoulder or lightly on the back of the neck. And though it may be viewed subserviently I like to open doors and pull out chairs. Communication has to be on point for these things to happen in public. There are many times she will submissively ask me something where she can't come outright and say it. If we are at a dinner and something is off her diet she will look at me with puppy eyes until I either nod or shake my head. And in that way we can maintain the dynamic and no one hardly knows what's happening.

In private its physically easier to make her feel owned and to be Dominant but at the same time its easier to let things slip. We maintain a touchy physical closeness. A lot of the gestures done in public won't work here as well. The subtlety comes off as too subtle. A pat on the ass or hug from behind is able to convey the same things that a hand on the back conveys in public. And I'm kind of a demanding fucker. I will plop my head or feet in her lap to rub them. At the same time she gets babied by getting her sore muscles rubbed and getting all the cuddles she can stand.

And in the bedroom is of course the least subtle and the area where most of us don't have to hold dominance back (within negotiation and consent of course!). To me, rope bondage is my best expression of dominance. For another Dominant it may be pain or verbal control. Those are the overarching things. But again a lot is done in the little details. And I usually discover these little things by accident. When I'm fucking her from behind and I have my hand tangled in her hair but I get tired and lean forward and push her head into the mattress. And she fucking loves it. Well that's a move now.

One thing in the bedroom that shows dominance like no other is moving her and putting her where you want her. Don't ask, don't demand. Pick her ass up and move her. If she's on her knees you can grab an ankle and flip her pretty easily If she's on her back slip a hand under her hip and flip her. And for girls that like it, grabbing a handful of hair and moving her where you need works too.

Dirty talk is another thing. I could do a whole article on dirty talk because it was a steep learning curve for me to get good and I can laugh at myself now. But asking questions and forcing her to say things can be just so hot and Dominant.

Another Dominant thing with a little primal mixed in is a hand on the throat. Now I don't mean breathplay though that is great as well. I mean just placing a hand there and letting her know you have that control. When angel lifts her head for me to put a hand on her throat I could not feel any more submitted to. Its like saying "here, you are in charge" (I'm the Captain now!).

The final thing is focus. This is hard to explain. And I have no idea why this gets pussies wet but it does. Being super focused while I'm tying or concentrating on some activity seems to just exude dominance to some people. Maybe its the fact that focus and attentiveness lets them feel safe enough to let go and be submissive. I'm not sure but its nice to hear, "you are so hot when you are focused".

Those are just some of the things I know and would give to a new Dominant in the form of advice. Everyone's mileage may vary. Not all dynamics will find these things useful. But for some they may be a good start.

A Dominant's True Power

In the six years I've been in "the Lifestyle" there has always been the debate about what makes a good (insert label of choice here). And I suspect as long as Fet exists there will always be debates about that sort of thing. Maybe I'm of a different mindset, but I've always believed that the dynamics were so complex that what made a good (insert label) for one person didn't necessarily make those qualities desirable for another person. For example, some Dom/mes love a sub that brats. Personally I do not. So a sub that brats constantly might make another Dom/me extremely happy but it won't me.

So while I believe that the dynamic is too complex to give a blanket "this is right" statement, there are some things that I believe are essential to making a good (insert label) in my eyes. These are things less like the posture of a sub in how they kneel or the skills of a Dom/me in swinging an impact toy. These are the personality traits that make that person capable of the things that others might see as good qualities.

And while I'd never presume to say what makes a good sub - because I like to adapt to what I'm given - I do know the qualities I try to embody to become the best Dom I can.

To that end, I believe that the Dominant's true power doesn't lie in these things:

*How hard or accurate they can swing.

*Having a commanding presence or booming voice.

*An alpha wolf personality that just oozes take charge ability.

It is my belief that a Dominant's true power comes from their ability to exercise control over their self.

For me, the Dominant's primary function is to ensure the people who rely on them are safe. So if the submissive wishes to be healthy and looks to the Dominant for leadership and help, and all they see is a lazy ass who stuffs their face with whatever junk is lying around, then they will remain unhealthy. If the submissive looks to the Dominant to ensure stability but they can't keep a job or honor commitments, then what kind of environment does that create?

The examples are numerous and applicable to each individual situation. But the point is still the same. How do wish to exercise or hold control over someone else if you can't control yourself?

Keep yourself in shape. You don't have to run miles or hit the gym. But do something to keep your body healthy.

Get regular checkups.

Meditate or do whatever you need to do to get your mind right. A Dominant with every skill who can't control their own emotions will find trouble.

Develop patience. Learn the ability to think before speaking.

Practice good hygiene. You should attempt to look as good if not better than your submissive at all times.

Conversely, I would caution submissives to consider any Dominant with the following qualities:

Inability to treat ex partners with respect. If your Dom/me's previous partners warn you - that's a red flag.

Asks you to do things they are incapable of doing. I don't mean that they won't let you tie them up. I mean they force your behavior (quit drinking, talk with respect, etc,.) when they can't abide by their own rules.

Doesn't learn. Everyone is human. Mistakes will be made. But the second time the situation comes up is there a change? Or just the same failure?

Being Primal

People are cautious of labels. It's easy to understand why. Labels are very confining and not in the good, "Oh I'm in bondage" kind of way. Rather they give some people, an easy way to form an impression of us without ever having to put in the work to get to know us.

For some people, a single label is pretty defining. There's nothing wrong with that. For other people, multiple labels aren't sufficient. But what happens when a label is so vague and undefining that its meaning is difficult to discern?

For me, the label of Primal is like this.

I'll preface by saying that I still wake up day to day trying to understand what it means to be Primal. It's also one of those labels that probably some people use just because it sounds cool and they get to identify with an animal. There's nothing wrong with that of course, to each his/her own.

I define it as this. There are things I logic out. I may plan a scene and decide that at 5 minutes in I'm going to choke her and also I may bite her. But there are other things that I Primal out. Which means that I don't really have to think about it. My lizard (or tiger) brain takes over, and I may have a plan in my head, but my primal side says, "Fuck your plan, man. Sink your teeth into her".

I don't know how it is for others but I can fight my primal side. Sometimes it's a lot of fun to draw out the hunting, seizing and claiming. Sometimes of course, the opposite is just as fun in its own way. To just let it out and see what debauched shit can happen.

I think that its also hard for some people to bring out their Primal side. Especially Dominants, we tend to fight the things that take control from us, even when they come from within. I think I spent years fighting it. And only with someone I felt absolute control with did I let that side express.

I used to go into the woods as a teenager and just strip naked. I thought it was some weird sex thing (well nothing's weird now), like exhibitionism, even though no one was around. It was letting the cool wind hit my skin and the squish of the soil and leaves between my toes and beneath my feet.

It's that overwhelming of the senses that happens. All senses have this need to be overwhelmed. I like to sniff my baby girl's scalp. I like to close my eyes and listen to the noises and sounds of sex. I like to feel things with all my parts. Primal is an amplification of everything around you.

On Sadism

I know you are testing me to see how sadistic I am...

When you call me:

*Mean
*Evil
*A "Bastard"
*Motherfucker
*Go to hell you fucking fucker
*Jerk

I know you intended for them to be insults. But all I hear are compliments. I smile and laugh and continue whatever sadistic behavior you are currently hating. I'm not sure if I'd love being a complete asshole to you if you enjoyed it. Maybe I would, but I'd find ways to make you not enjoy it.

Whether I'm getting you worked up and wet by mindfucking you and then not allowing you to cum when you ask.

Whether I'm using the whip to crack the same spot on your ass over and over and over again.

Whether I'm running the wartenberg wheel over the same nipple for the 17th time in a row.

Whether I'm pretending to ignore your signals to try and get me to fuck you now and hard.

When you can call me anything...please don't call me sweet things like sugar and honey and baby and other saccharine misnomers.

Call me the most hateful things you can through gritted teeth so I can hear how much you love me.

Rope Primer

Rope is one of our favorite activities to do. So I wrote up a quick primer for those interested in trying rope.

Safety

The sexiest questions people ask are about safety. How to do rope safely is always challenging, but very possible. Go slowly. That's my mantra. Every time I've tried to push things too far too fast, something happened. Now, I don't have anything more than a little slip here or there to remind me that I'm human and not superhuman.

Always keep EMT shears close by when tying. Never be afraid to cut rope. I've never actually cut it but I've had the scissors in my hand before. Nerve damage is the primary concern. Educate yourself on the nerves in the body and learn to avoid hurting them. But also know the precursor signs to nerve damage and communicate them to your bottom.

And lastly I make it habit not to tie necks. Yes, I have done it. But I am in control of the rope at all times and I control the pressure. If she were to fall over the rope would slip through my hands. NEVER tie off a neck rope to anything. And if you are a beginner - get your double columns and futomomo ties down first and keep the neck ropes for later - or never.

Communication

This is one of the most paramount points when doing rope and ties (pun not intended) right back to safety. If you find that you or your bottom are thoroughly incapable of communication, then one or both of you need to be ready to walk away or someone will very likely end up fucked up physically or mentally. This is also why I don't tie people I don't know or at least have some level of trust with. Of course, this can be alleviated if my bottom is around to guide the other person.

Equipment

The most common question is about type of rope. I used to recommend the clothesline from Lowes. But after processing raw hemp from Rawganique.com, I have changed my mind. For about $30 you can get enough raw hemp rope to do pretty much any tie. And the processing is a meditative event. I like hemp. It will always be my favorite. I like 6mm for lots of things. However I still maintain that 8mm works best for suspension and for bigger bodies. That's my preference although I realize not everyone agrees with me. I even have a little bit of 4mm hemp for tying smaller body parts. If you want processed, dyed hemp, I think TwistedMonk.com is a great source.

Jute is my second favorite. While hemp is pretty stiff in most cases unless really worn in, jute is kind of floppy. It's a little tougher to tie in my opinion, but it holds knots well and it "bites". If I want to leave marks, I'll use jute. I like MyNawashi on Etsy for a source.

If you want the rope to look pretty, the nylon stuff that is put out by Knothead Nylon looks great. I've never used it though so I can't testify to its other properties.

Learning

I think there are several choices for learning and I think that one would be well advised to utilize every single source they can.

The first would be a good mentor. I never really had a mentor for rope when I was getting into this. I just stumbled my way through. It can be kind of difficult, because if you find a rope mentor in your area they can be guarded about having competition. But for me, I find that being a mentor in the small ways I have so far gives me a lot of joy and it actually helps me put things in perspective.

There are also a lot of good videos on the web. My personal favorites are those by Two Knotty Boys and Twisted Monk. Both can be found on Youtube. In addition to the videos there are books for the "slow" learning. Its easier for me sometimes to see it in steps in a book. Two Knotty Boys have two excellent books and the Douglas Kent Shibari series is also excellent.

Practice

I'm a sadist who tries his tools out on himself first. I like to know what they feel like. Therefore I recommend self-tying first and foremost. Now some Rope Tops and Doms will say - NO WAY! But the truth is that until you know how it feels you won't know how it feels on someone else. Tying without self-tying is like having sex and THEN discovering masturbation. This will let you play with tightness and tensions and wraps. You won't be able to do every tie on yourself, but you can get started. Plus, would you really want your first fumbly time to be with a hot body who volunteered to be your rope bottom?

After self-tying of course, the goal is to tie real people. Find someone you trust and have a connection with. Someone you can learn with. A good rope bottom will make a decent Rope Top look really good. When practicing, I like to take the sex out of it. It's understood that no sex will occur. I mean that's always a good practice with a new rope bottom, but I still do this with my babygirl and partner of 3 years now. It's hard to focus on two things at once. I find it much safer and better to practice with sex off the table.

I get the question all the time - where do I find someone to tie? You have the greatest kink website in history available to find people. Post pics of your work. Study up. Get good at self-ties and learn. People will naturally find you and want to be tied.

Goal

This is the one thing that people don't really think about when they start tying. What is your goal? Do you think rope looks pretty? Is it a puzzle (one person told me this and it was like wow, awesome!)? Do you want to torture a masochist? Do you want to have (consensual) sex with your bottom? When setting up a scene, if you don't think about these things and make the right choices, it will backfire on you. You'll end up with a bottom who has every fun place tied off. So think about what the end goal is in a scene (which can change day to day as long as communication happens).

Aftercare

Taking someone out of rope is an act unto itself. Some people like to pull ropes off themselves. These are called "ex-play partners". Seriously. The rope should be removed slowly unless it's done as a torture act. Limbs will be stiff and bloodflow is returning. Trying to jerk rope from limbs can cause other issues.

Then aftercare should be given of course. I find that people like to be told they did a good job. This isn't the time for critique or problem solving.

This is not comprehensive and I will add to it as I can. Suggestions are welcome.

A Quiet Dominance

When I first found out I was Dominant, I was not quiet. I was a loudmouth idiot trained by what TV and film and erotica thought a Dom should be. I was a giant walking bag of expletives. Bitch this. Whore that. Slut slut slut. Fucking cunt. Filthy dumb fucking slut whore cunt bitch. Go here! Do this! Now! Now! Now! I imagine if I could look back at myself through a time machine, I would laugh at all the douchiness.

I don't judge people who like to talk a lot. If that's their kink, then that's great. A lot partners like that kind of talk. I especially like degradation and verbal tasks that cause the submissive to struggle. Particularly questions they can't answer easily or have to think about while being totally distracted. But that's not what I'm talking about here.

I'm talking about the laughable, scripted talk that a Dominant might think they are required to spew in order to get a submissive to comply. I think having to be loud and forceful to a submissive has fail written all over it. Again, if that's your thing - no offense intended.

But I still laugh, because I think that sometimes the severity of the words and the verbose nature of the Dominant belies a lack of confidence. Like if they are just harsh enough, my words will have the meaning that I want. And it's true, sometimes harsh words are all we have. But they shouldn't be the ONLY tool.

Myself, I enjoy being a more quiet Dominant. I feel it has more meaning. I feel that a stern look and strong eye contact along with hand gestures show a confident spirit. And don't forget about manhandling. I think the pinnacle of confidence is not telling a submissive to get into a position, pose or stance but rather to move them directly to it. But even something like manhandling can be done loudly. There's a kind of poetry to simplicity; to moving a submissive with a single push or pull.

When talking occurs I think it should be confident, forceful, direct and clear. Loud is only necessary with hard of hearing submissives, and I bet it is just entertaining to a brat.

Nurturing Does Not Equal Weak

Even with labels, there are varying levels of personality that go with each. This means that every Dominant won't be right for every submissive and vice versa. It's a constant learning process to discover what we like and what type of person fits us best.

Which is why it constantly astounds me when people exclude a certain label or personality because it doesn't fit the fantasy of what they imagine. I'm no less guilty of these things. I excluded Daddy for years because I didn't understand it, or didn't want to. I was comfortable in my little Master bubble even though that label didn't fit me at all.

But it is irritating when those fantasies actually interfere with otherwise good dynamics. I think this is very clear when a nurturing Dominant is thought of as weak.

As far as nurturing Dominants, I don't mean just Daddy/Mommy. I mean Dominants who have a pragmatic view of things. And this is why I think dynamics sometimes fail. You get a submissive who says they crave strict, harsh Dominance and a Dominant who feels they must live up to that ideal. When the first life event comes up and D feels they can't relent even though s needs some nurturing but all of a sudden the dynamic breaks and each are pointing fingers.

Nurturing does not equal weak. I'll put rules in place. I'll enforce them. I'll punish and reward accordingly. My sadist will beat your fucking ass and I'll laugh and enjoy it.

But when I don't come down extra hard, it doesn't mean I'm weak. It means I'm human and I will adapt to what you need in the moment and not become some idealistic robot devoid of emotion.

Being a little

Introduction

Ew, I bet you have Daddy issues...

You call your boyfriend "Daddy" what the fuck is wrong with you?

You're childish, infantile, and irresponsible because you're little...

Will you grow up already?

Did you really bring a bear to the dentist?

"That's why I won't (insert action here) with littles..."

Being "little" does not mean you have Daddy issues. I have a wonderful healthy relationship with my Father. I call my boyfriend Daddy because it makes us fucking happy. He takes care of me in every way possible. He helps me be the best me that I can be. That doesn't mean I have no responsibility, or that I am incapable of being an adult when I need to be. I worked in EMS for 16years; I never once had a moment where I wasn't a strong woman kicking ass and taking names daily. I have two step kiddos that I take care of, and I help Daddy on the farm. All that being said, I just love my little to pieces, and there is nothing wrong with being little.

My "little" is the part of me that hasn't become bitter over the world, or the things I've experienced in my life. It's the part of me that looks at life and embraces all that is good. The simplest of things can bring such joy to my heart. Going to the nature reserve and seeing all the animals. When Daddy takes me to the aquarium and I can see all my favorite fishies. When He takes me to the arcade and lets me win at air hockey even though I gloat lol.

My littlespace is when I can be silly and carefree. When I can let go of all the icky adulty things I have to do everyday and climb up in Daddy's lap for snuggles. The big smile on my face when he makes my favorite snack, ants on apples instead of logs, and i get peanut butter all over my fingers. Spending an hour picking out the best colors for a picture I'm making to tell Daddy "thank you for loving me as I am". It's wearing my sparkly unicorn shirt, sequined backpack, and glittered kicks and knowing Daddy thinks I'm adorable. It's watching all those movies I grew up with over and over again until Daddy can sing all the songs with me.

Having my Daddy means I have someone to cling to when the thunder claps at 3:00am and I'm terrified. It means having someone take me and bearbear to the dentist and not giving a fuck if people look at his babygirl strangely. It's having someone remind you of goals you set for yourself, pushing you to achieve them, and still making it fun. It's having a partner who accepts every side of you, big or small, and encouraging you to express yourself.

Identifying as or being with a little isn't for everyone. I am a lot of work, but I have a huge heart, and love with every inch of it. For some people I am a catch. There is nothing wrong with me because I'm a little, and there is nothing wrong with you either. Don't allow the judgement or snarky comments of other force your little into hiding. Someone out there is just dying to have a little like you.

The little as Alter Ego

I think it's easy to imagine the transformation from a regular person into a little as some marked event where there's a clear line from adult person to little. Almost like when Clark Kent ran into the phone booth and Superman emerged. There's a clear line in time where one persona left and the other one began again.

But from talking to so many littles, and living with one for several years now I can tell you, no clear line of demarcation exists. It's not a simple thing that a person can just bring out. Superman only hides as Clark Kent because he wants to. Many littles hide because they feel they have to.

There are many reasons I've been told that littles hide. A spouse or parent or family member disapproves. The little side has been betrayed or hurt or aware of societal pressures. Etc. This is just the reality.

What's more is that as I mentioned, that clear line doesn't exist so sometimes it's hard to recognize when the little emerges. There's no shiny suit they wear as they remove their big glasses. There's no pretty butterfly flying out of the cocoon.

I think as Daddies, there are a few things we can do to nurture the emergence. For one, we can be very observant in order to recognize when our littles emerge. Because they can be driven back in VERY easily. A harsh word or a different attitude and the little is gone.

In the same vein, littles can work out a signal to their Daddy. It may be a tone change in voice or hair in pigtails or what have you. Just something that signals, "hey, little me is here". I know for us this works, when we both remember the signal anyway.

Creating a safe place for a little to emerge is important too. We have to sometimes pick up a chore or do something nice to bring that little side out.

I find myself frequently asked by littles how they can make that side emerge.

*Buying something nice and little (gummies, coloring books, a movie).
*Doing something a little would like (tickle fights, cooking together, etc.).
*Touching the way a little would want (petting head, brushing hair, giving a bath).
*Removing all other distractions. As I mentioned, making sure we have quiet alone time.
*Being silly.

How do you littles bring your little side out?

My "little" Side, And What the Term "Daddy" Means To Me

By @CuriousKitty009

I know a lot of littles, and most are very in tune with their younger inner selves. Many of them color, play with stuffies, use a pacifier, and do littles-oriented activities. It can be fun to interact with them, but I often feel disconnected in that environment. For me, my "little" is more of a "middle". I am more independent than a younger-identifying little. I have some little qualities, like wearing babydoll lingerie and onesies, playing a brat for fun, and getting into general mischief.

But more than anything, my little side represents my vulnerability. My emotional side, the part of me that needs protection, guidance, nurturing. It is not sexual in nature, but it is also not innocent. My little side comes out when I'm hurt, or scared, or worried. It craves cuddles, and comfort... a loving pair of arms wrapped around me, fingers running through my hair, a hand wiping away my tears, caring eyes looking into mine, telling me everything will be alright.

For me, the word "Daddy" takes on a different meaning than most. Sure, I can use it as a form of roleplay during sex, but I'm not typically one to play up the whole age difference thing, or feign innocence in an ageplay kind of way - the concept of "Daddy" taking away my innocence isn't appealing to me. For a long time, I couldn't even bring myself to use that word in the bedroom. But over time, there have been

instances of where it can be fun. That said, my definition of "Daddy" in the bedroom is a completely different context than that of a D/s relationship.
In my definition of a DD/lg D/s, "Daddy" means protector, guardian, mentor, caretaker, lover, and Dominant.

Someone who earns the **title** of Daddy has earned my trust. He keeps me safe, has my best interests at heart, and strives to help me grow. He sees me not only as his little girl, but also as his partner. He recognizes my strengths, and utilizes them to form a bond between us deeper than any other I've experienced. He knows my deepest, darkest secrets, because I volunteer them freely to him. He understands my desires, because he actively seeks them out, coaxing and pushing my boundaries. He punishes me, not out of frustration, but to satisfy my need for stability and structure. He praises me when I please him, or accomplish something for myself. He tells me why he loves me. He does little things to remind me how much he cares. He is firm, but forgiving. He accepts when I make mistakes, and talks about them together. He sees me for who I am, inside and out, and he loves me unconditionally.
I'm still looking for my Daddy. I hope that's he's also out there, looking for me...

The Importance of Laughter in Big/little Relationships

By @IADaddyMaster

A while back I was asked the following questions, "Define little. Why do you like them?"

I think the most basic definition if a little is someone who is younger in mind and spirit than their physical age would indicate. For some littles this is through regression and for others it is just the way they are wired. It rather corresponds to my own outlook which can be summed up in this quote, "being a kid versus being an adult is not an either-or choice, it is simply a matter of time and place." And I try to live by that maxim, never forgetting the unbridled joy of watching a butterfly, jumping in a puddle, or dancing in the rain. And I think for most littles that is a constant state of being.

I think there are two things, I particularly like about littles. The first is simply the joie de vivre. It matches very well with my own outlook on life. I am happy to spend time coloring with my little or snuggled up in a blanket fort. I have a very youthful outlook on life and I like that reflected in my partner. The other reason is the deep level of power exchange that is inherent in the Daddy/little dynamic. I enjoy the control and the ownership. But at the same time, I enjoy taking care of my partner and guiding them. I am often asked about how I see that in terms of also being a master and enjoying the master/slave dynamic. To me they are really just two sides of the same coin. And all the things that go with being a master and taking ownership of another person apply equally well to being a daddy. They are both deep levels of power exchange and to me represent what both should be at their best.

Now you might be wondering what any of this has to do with laughter. Well if goes back to the point about being a kid vs being an adult. I am firmly convinced that the best daddies/mommies/caregivers are the ones that let their inner child out to play right along with their little. I often say about myself that right alongside the "Parental Advisory" sticker I am required to wear, I should be required to wear another one that says "Adult Supervision Required".

My playfulness shows in many ways. I am a fond connoisseur of horrible puns and dad jokes. They usually leave my little rolling on the floor laughing until they have tears running down their face. I am a master of making silly songs and even sillier poetry. I am happy to sit on the floor and color with my little or have a tea party. If they want to make a blanket fort and snuggle away in it while we watch a princess movie, I will be right there beside them. And in my case trying crazy things in the kitchen like trying to make homemade cheese and have them help. I like to do these things not just because they bring joy to my little but because I genuinely like being a kid myself sometimes.

And in addition to the joy, it helps my little feel more at ease about being little. They can let go more easily of all they adult things and become playful, silly, and small when they see me being just as silly and goofy. It makes them feel better about themselves and their desire to be little. And the more at ease they are with themselves and all the aspects of who they are, the happier and healthier a little will be. It makes it safe for them be everything that they are and not keep it bottled up inside them.

Finally, and arguably most important, the silliness we share strengthens the bonds between us. It gives us one more area where we can share and collaborate. We can spend more time directly engaged in activities and with each other. The more time we spend in these shared moments the stronger and more durable the ties between us become and the more resilient we are as a couple. It is the strong bonds which sustain us when times are not as good and the world is pressing down on one or both of us. It gives us something to look forward to and allows us both to escape for a while into our special place.

Patience In Finding a Daddy

I find that the older I get, the harder it is to be patient for the things I need or want. Nothing rang more true than when I finally realized who I was inside, and the life I needed to live to be happy. I was kinky damn it, and I wasn't going to hide it anymore. I needed a Daddy, and I was searching everywhere for him.

I became so enamored with the thought of my Daddy being out there, that I began to overlook things that were important to me, just for the sake of having one. I allowed myself to be vulnerable with strangers thinking if I just opened up, that they could be what I needed. I was lied to, manipulated, cheated on, and often felt abandoned. I was called needy. I was hurt over and over again, and I couldn't figure out why. I was about to give up and walk away from "the Lifestyle" all together.

I FINALLY realized that the problem was me. I was the common denominator, and my impatient frenzy to find my Dominant clouded my judgement. It was in that moment of clarity I learned to slow down. Then one day in the settled dust, He found me. I no longer had to try make pieces fit where they didn't. I spent a lot of time getting to know Him. I was cautious, timid, afraid for the other shoe to drop, but it never did. He was my perfect.

For once in my life I was patient and allowed the relationship to progress organically. Yes, there was work put into creating our life together, but I didn't try to force it into something it wasn't. He naturally became my everything. We didn't have to drastically change each other to make our relationship successful. Just an expression of need from the other was enough to encourage a little change. Even though we aren't directly responsible for the others happiness, we do what we can to keep each other fulfilled.

Patience is one of the hardest qualities to practice. We all want what we want when we want it, and in this frenzy to fulfill our desires we often set ourselves up for heartbreak. Take your time when cultivating new relationships. Don't just go through the motions and progress the way you think other couples have. Be true to who you are, what you want, and what you need.

Being Needy

I absolutely detest the phrase, "He/She is just too needy". We are emotional creatures, and every single one of us has a list of needs to be met to achieve happiness. When someone says, "Well they were just too needy, and I couldn't deal with them", it is putting blame on that person for being human. It's wrong.

I was called needy in previous relationships, and it took me some time to realize that those words were nothing but an excuse. It was an attempt to gaslight my feelings and needs so they could get what they wanted for as long as they wanted it. We are conditioned to look at having needs as a bad thing, and it's just not true. It wasn't until I met my Daddy that I realized I wasn't "needy" at all, I just hadn't found someone who WANTED to make me happy.

If someone calls you "needy" they are really saying, "I don't have the time, energy, or desire to try to make you happy". If people are honest about what they are able to contribute to a relationship instead of using the word "needy", then we could start to remove the negative connotation associated with that word.

Relationships are one of the hardest things people will navigate through their lives. They require so much communication and honesty to make things work. If you have one person always saying what they need and the other refuses to discuss it or even try to, it will seem as if the person making the effort to establish communication is needy.

So to recap.. It is not okay to call someone "needy". It is an excuse. What is okay is honestly telling someone that what they need, and what you are capable of giving are not in alignment and go your separate ways without the shame and guilt.

Too Old to little

Being a part of the community can be both daunting and amazing when it comes to the process of aging. As a little I find this process to be one of the most difficult things to go through.

My outside is 36. My skin is getting looser. I have wrinkles around my eyes. Things that sat up at attention are now a little more floppy. I find it harder to get away with expressing myself the way I need to. I like having pretty colors or feathers in my hair. I love my pink sequined unicorn backpack. My rainbow socks and red kicks put an extra bounce in my step. These things make me happy, but sometimes people look at me strangely. It makes me worry that I'm too old to be a little.

During those darker times I have the WOMEN of my community to turn to, and it's a blessing. Beautiful women who proudly throw on a onesie and rock some piggy tails. Women who confidently embrace who they are, and hide for no one. I am thankful for all of you because it gives me the confidence to be true to myself.

On the flip side of the coin are the beautiful young girls. I see their perfect little bodies, and all the adorable cutie things they wear, and it makes me melancholy. It's a brief pang of mixed emotions. Mostly of regret. I regret not embracing my little and being who I was for so long. So many of my years were spent hiding my little in fear of judgement. Then there is pride. I'm proud of these girls for expressing who they are. For living the life they need and being strong.

My hope is that in 10 years, when I'm probably too old to be little, they will see me still being true to myself. That maybe I'll become the woman that inspires them to stay little even when it gets overwhelming. That they will be confident to continue their journey when they are 36 because being little has nothing to do with our outer shells, and everything to do with our little hearts.

Disclaimers

Fake Daddies

I try to steer away from calling anyone fake or criticizing anyone's dynamic. Since I've been active I've seen things that I didn't think were right but later found out that between two consenting adults as long as its legal then who am I to criticize.

However the one thing that still rubs me raw is people who pick up submissives, get them to submit and then break them just for the fun of it. And in no dynamic is this any more obvious than with the DD/lg dynamic. For the purpose of this writing I'm ignoring genders because I'm sure they all do this.

I'm sure this doesn't always happen on purpose. Littles sometimes hide and then once they get to know a person they reveal all of themselves. This is not unusual and it's a bad cycle of hiding, revealing and getting hurt that continues to spiral. For me that's why it's important to ask the right questions up front.

But for me, fake daddies (lowercase on purpose) actually become submissives in the relationship. And there's no amount of sadistic beating or barking orders that will make them anything but submissives. They become submissive because they change their nature to get sex and companionship out of a person. They pretend to be something they are not because they see that as their only desperate chance to get what they want.

In a lot of relationships, sex has a diminishing rate of return. And the pretending that one might do to get sex will eventually become more work for them than the sex is worth.

I've heard of daddies asking the little to take the dynamic out of it and just have sex. This is a warning sign. A Daddy asks for the dynamic to be more present. A daddy asks for a break from it.

Why Littles Have a Tough Time

Until I met my babygirl I had no idea what a Daddy or babygirl even was. I had the notions an outsider does and thought none of it was for me. But like most things - special people that you meet make you better. I heard horror stories and not just from my babygirl - from others as well.

Abandonment. Overly harsh punishments. A total lack of understanding of the dynamic.

Now I'm not one to judge. I had to learn how to be this. Granted, I think some of it was inherent. If a dynamic works for two people and there is consent I say go for it!

But littles have a tougher time for a few reasons:

1. They trust too easily. When you break it down, you have a grown person who has the same sexual and emotional needs as the rest of us. But that person also likes to revert and be carefree and young. And that often comes a bit of naïveté.

2. They see the best in people. Like a child can't see the evil in the world, neither can a little.

3. The things they fear make them more willing to overlook bad qualities. Once a little attaches they fear abandonment above all else. So rather than be abandoned they will eat all manner of shit just to hang on.

As Daddies we can do things to make sure we are prepared.

1. If you don't think you are cut out to Daddy then step aside.

2. If you don't think you are cut out to Daddy then STEP ASIDE.

3. If you don't think you are cut out to Daddy THEN STEP ASIDE. Seriously. The thought of fucking a young hot girl who calls you Daddy is close to irresistible. If you are a mental sadist or a master manipulator, you won't heed this message, but you are probably not cut out to Daddy. And while it would be a great world if we self-policed, it's probably not going to happen.

Daddies, Please be Careful

Being a Daddy is such a big responsibility, and not every man is strong enough to be a good one. As a little, I just wish they would think about what it really means to be a Daddy and have a little before they get into that type of relationship.

They need to be strong, patient, nurturing, attentive and affectionate, kind hearted, open, honest, yet still firm. In return, they get a babygirl who always looks at him with love in her eyes. A devotion that is unshakeable by any other. A baby who wants nothing more than to make Daddy happy in every way she can. He's her own personal hero, and even though she may be sensitive - she is his rock. The one person in this world that will always be there to keep him grounded when he needs to be. To give him cuddles and love when he needs it, and build him up as much as he builds her up.

A Daddy's heart is just as important as our little hearts. It is definitely a relationship that takes trust, and loyalty. Daddy is the one man in our lives that we should be able to put on a pedestal and love without being destroyed. Men!!! If you don't understand what it truly means to be a Daddy and love a little, then please don't claim to be one. Our happiness is in your strong hands - don't take that for granted. Need us as much as we need you. Love us as much as we love you. Cherish all our moments together. The silly ones when we are both giggling together, the happy ones where we are content in each other's arms, the dirty ones when Daddy takes us to a place we didn't know before, the rough times when we need your guidance and wisdom, and the mushy ones that make us yours completely. We will always be your good little girls if you are a good Daddy to us.

I just wanted to express what a relationship like this really means to us. It, and you are our everything. A strong and wonderful Daddy is hard to come by. So littles, if you find him, then never, ever let him have to second guess your devotion to him. Make sure he always knows he's the most important man in your life, and put as much effort into his happiness as they put into ours.

Being a Daddy is Not Easy

It is not my intention to garner sympathy. I love being a Daddy and would not change that for anything. But it is not easy.

I did not know I was a Daddy until I met her. I had known I was Dominant for several years but something always felt missing. None of the BDSM books about it in general really cover Daddy Dom in more than a cursory way. If not for her, somedays I wonder if I'd ever know who I truly was.

But again, it is not easy.

Daddies care for a little (sometimes more than one). It can be tough caring for more than one person. And I don't mean two littles. The Daddy has to care for himself too. And if that Daddy has children (actual children) then that adds to everything. Add a job, parents, bills, etc. It can be a little overwhelming.

A Daddy has to, all at once, care about the day and make it fun and happy for a little and also worry about the future. They end up having a foot in both realms. Pay too little attention to today and the little is less than happy and you won't get to enjoy that side. Pay too little attention to the future and you may not be able to provide or even have a little to provide for.

Daddies tend to internalize every little problem.

Telling a little "no" is part of the job, but some of us hate doing that. At the same time, failing to take care of our little by keeping the rules is also a huge fault. I wonder often which is more damaging - the "no" or her seeing me fail to keep the rules. I've never been the 24/7 strict Master type and I know that about myself.

I hope this doesn't come off as a "woe is me" type writing. I would take 100 times this to be with my babygirl. She is worth walking through fire.

So it's not easy. Which is why I think many Dominants want to take that leap into being a "Big" but find themselves failing after just a little bit. It's not that they aren't good enough as a Dominant or that the little isn't worth it. It's just that sometimes the walls press in pretty hard. It sucks that a little has to be the crash test dummy. Which is why I preach caution in starting those types of relationships if either party is new to that dynamic.

Don't Pay Lip Service to Gaining a little's Trust

There are a lot of writings on about trust in the DD/lg and similar dynamics. Writers will talk about how important trust is and how bad it is to break that trust. But I feel like we pay a lot of lip service to trust without actually talking about how it's earned or lost. So for a new Daddy/Mommy Dominant there's no good starting point. And I realize that giving information on trust is going to attract predators but newsflash - they already know how to gain trust so they can abuse it.

Create a safe haven

I've never met a little who wasn't shy. I've met very few who haven't been hurt whether intentionally or on accident. It's a huge ego blow, but even the best Daddy Dom won't meet a little's little on the first meeting in most cases. Probably more than with any other kink dynamics, littles get shamed for who they are. "Why can't you be an adult?" "A pacifier, really?". People just don't understand. I've had to explain things to my parents who don't care to understand our dynamic. But I explain it in such a way that I don't find it abnormal so they shouldn't either. So they ask the question, I answer and we move on.

The point is that you have to create a safe haven for the little to come out. This is more than just buying coloring books and keeping cartoon movies. Littles peek out slowly, more and more. You have to be extra careful not only to create an environment where they feel mentally safe to come out, but you also have to not push them back in.

I find that many littles are extremely self-aware that when they come out, a D-type who isn't patient or strong may find the little part grating or annoying. So they hide it so they aren't irritating to their D-type. This goes away in time. But even a good D-type will say or do something, not realizing it's to the little side, and drive the little side back down for a bit.

So you have to create a place where the little wants to come out. This is a place with a Dominant who is welcoming and able to meet the needs of the little without making them feel ashamed or judged. If you feel ashamed or annoyed or embarrassed or weird, then they will too.

Be of your word

In this dynamic, as in life, things happen. Just because we are part of a different dynamic doesn't mean that life events won't interfere. And these will sometimes get in the way of said dynamic. These are understandable occurrences. However, if you want to see a little be themself you have to keep your word to them. It helps to look at a little as a magical creature who feeds on Daddy/Mommy energy. When their D-type doesn't show up, the spell loses its power.

It's important to not make promises if the potential for not keeping them is high. Don't set up a plan that is destined to fail. It's ok to tell a little "no", and in fact momentary disappointment is way better than driving one back down by not keeping your word.

Develop patience

For me, when I talk to littles and hear that their Daddy or Mommy asked them to turn their little off, I find that to be a HUGE red flag. I'm sure the D-type wouldn't like to be told to turn their Dominant off or turn their gender or intelligence or anything else off. A little has that part of their personality. It's not something they do to have fun or as a hobby. It's part of them. Asking them to turn it off is like asking them to wear a mask.

But, this is a sign of a D-type lacking patience. They feel like they need a break and that they can't handle their little. The truth is that they probably aren't well suited for a little, or not the type of little that they are with at the very least. It helps to have patience. All littles want to buy fun stuff and do things we may not be super interested in doing, or they may be extra clingy. We should view these as good things and not annoyances.

In the end, some people are not cut out to be a Daddy and do it where it's not going to hurt a little. It's best if these people recognize their flaws and work on them. Even people who are cut out for it can do well to find flaws and fix them. But not changing and not adapting is hurting people that they claim to care about. Trust can be earned and will be well rewarded, but you have to actively seek it and work toward it.

Negotiation and Consent

Ethical Negotiation

I hate the term "ethical". The reason is because it's subjective. What is the definition of ethical? Well, doing things right. Who defines what is right?

I once worked for a company that had a huge display about ethics in their lobby. We are an ethical company. We only do things the right way. We treat people right. I worked there for one year on contract before I purposely let my contract expire. During that time I'd been asked to forge documents, lie to customers, allow shoddy product into the field, do silly accounting tricks to hide money and not pay contractors. But they were happy that they were so ETHICAL.

Now that I've gotten out the way my utter contempt for that word.

Ethical negotiation to me as applied very narrowly and specifically to needle play (say for a scene):

Bottom: I like needles. I'd like you to put them in me.

Top: I like needles as well. I would like to put them in you. Here are some things I do to make sure they are safe. You know infection is a risk, right?

Bottom: That sounds great. I'd like you to put them in me. Here are the places that are ok and not ok.

Top: Awesome.

Here's an unethical negotiation:

Top: I like needles.

Bottom: I don't like them.

Top: Well once I get you tied down I'm going to put them in anyway.

Bottom: That's not cool.

Top: Well if you really liked me you'd let me do it. And if you don't let me I'll tell everyone you slept with Jim last week and everyone knows Jim has the clap.

So two widely different ends of the spectrum.

Here's one that most people seem to have trouble with:

Top: I like needles.

Bottom: I don't get off on the pain. However I have always wanted to do needles and I think it would be cool if I could suffer through that with you.

Top: Are you sure? If needles aren't your thing...

Bottom: I'm asking you to please do them with me. I consent to them.

Top: There's a small risk of infection.

Bottom: Yes I'm aware. I still want to do it.

{So the scene happens and Top compliments bottom}

Top: Thank you. You did such a good job. Thank you for suffering through that.

Bottom: I enjoyed suffering through it. It turned me on to be able to do that.

Now you can be very vanilla and focus on the act itself. These people are FUCKING CRAZY. Who would stick needles in someone else? He must be abusing her. Because very clearly she didn't want needles (though she asked twice and clarified she wanted needles).

What separates what we do from abuse?

Negotiation, consent and safewords.

Negotiation is the speed limit everyone agrees to when they get on the road.

Consent is the driver's license that allows you to drive on the road.

Safewords are yellow and red lights.

A Plea To Vanilla Spouses

Dear Vanilla Spouse,

Can you spare 5 minutes to read this and save your marriage? Perhaps not. Life is busy. You are married. They aren't going anywhere. There's too much history between you two. You have kids and a house and a business together for fuck's sake.

You are comfortable in your marriage of 2, 5, 10, 15, 25 years. You both married each other for good reasons. You've been together for a long time for equally good reasons. Why is any change necessary?

It's very likely they didn't know they were kinky. It took a(n) (in)famous book or a movie or a website stumbled upon way late at night in error. And they stayed up half the night absorbing this world like a sponge. They didn't want to be kinky. They didn't want to upset the applecart. But they are. The cat's out of the bag. Pandora's box is open.

Your complete and utter lack of interest shows. You don't have to take on the role they want. We believe in consent and limits. But just ignoring everything and not at least talking about common ground or finding solutions? Well that's careless. That's foolhardy. It wasn't a vanilla wife who broke my marriage. It was a disinterested one.

Perhaps it's hard to see the shoe on the other foot. Have they ever done anything for you just to be a giver? They wash your dirty ass underwear. Go work a dangerous job to make ends meet. Get along with your parents.

You don't have to sell your morals down the road. You don't have to buy into all of this. You don't have to really do a goddamn thing. But you are going to lose the one you love. Maybe they don't walk out the door tomorrow. Maybe it happens in steps and degrees. Maybe they stay and never go anywhere. But you've lost them all the same.

Call it atrophy. Call it failure to evolve. But it's really a lack of imagination.

Don't offer to change as they have one foot out the door. You can't only want something once you realize its gone.

Sincerely,

Someone Trying to Help

Stopping At No

I've never had a safeword used on me. Not once in the 7 years since I started doing this. So I get a cookie, right? Hardly.

I'm the kind of Dominant - and I know plenty more like me - who stops at "ouch", "no", "don't" or any other word that indicates my submissive is not "feeling it". We aren't special. We are probably the Dominants who get a reputation for being wimps or not taking it far enough Again, I couldn't care much. We don't stop because we worry about consent violation claims or anything other than we just want to do a good job. I would rather hear "I could have taken more" than "You gave me too much".

I agree with her 100% because she knows that if she failed to use a safeword with me and needed to, and should have then there would be serious repercussions; and no matter how much I love her it would severely hamper my ability to confidently do kink with her in the future. THE SAFEWORD IS THERE FOR A GODDAMNED REASON. It's to protect all parties involved. Red works in our house whether we are kissing or cooking dinner.

D or s, if you consider play and the other person says any of the following:

*I don't do safewords.
*I don't do aftercare.
*I don't believe in consent.
*Don't stop no matter what I say.
*You can't hurt me.

RUN FAR. RUN FAST. I don't care how beautiful they are. How special or respected they are. They aren't worth playing with.

Talk Until The Sexy Is Gone

When I first started into BDSM, my mentor said something that made no sense to me. I was asking how I would know what to do. I mean seriously. When you have no exposure and don't know that resources like Fetlife or this book are available you will be lost.

"Well what does she like?" she asked.

"No fucking clue." I typed.

"Talk about what you each like. Talk until the sexy is gone."

And that stuck with me. It drives other people crazy, but I like to talk until the sexy is gone and then beyond. I can't help but think that if we did more of this in the BDSM community, that we'd see the misunderstandings that cause consent violations go away.

I think it's important to talk until the sexy is gone for two reasons.

The first reason is that I can be hit or miss sexy with you right now or I can be 100% sexy (well maybe 92% lol) later. I'm not even going to get to 75% without talking and getting to know what someone likes.

When I first met her I'd ask what she wanted. She'd talk to me for a little bit and then say, "just let it happen organically". It would drive me crazy. I'm a planner and I'll obsess over a scene for hours, until I know exactly how everything is going to go and what every backup plan is.

And it seems like everyone we talk to when we ask what they like they have no idea. And it's because no one ever asked them. Then when we are good they are shocked. Like, we didn't just know what you wanted. We picked and picked and picked. Talked until the sexy was gone and THEN we acted upon the information.

The second, more important reason, is that you don't violate consent or hard limits. I'm shocked by the stories I hear when someone says something is a limit and the other person doesn't ask for clarification. It's quite Dominant to ask a submissive to clarify a limit. "Please clarify..." It means you care enough to ask.

And if the person you are asking for clarification from won't elaborate, then play should not happen. That's my opinion. When you are talking about emotionally scarring someone (or your damn self) isn't a few words worth it?

The thing about language is that it isn't 100% effective.

Making the Dynamic Work

Dynamics Are Like Any Relationship

When you go to an all you can eat buffet you can ignore the healthy stuff. Personally, I skip the salad bar because I'm a meat and potatoes kind of guy. And I have a major sweet tooth.

It's not the same way with a D/s dynamic. You can negotiate things and set limits but if you ignore the broccoli and greens of the dynamic for the chocolate cake you will find that you are poisoning the dynamic the same as you are poisoning your body with the sweets.

I hear the common lament: "I can't find a Dom/Daddy/slave/babygirl/Master (insert other label)."

Also: "Why can't I find someone who wants to do X but not Y?"

Now I'm not saying anyone has to do anything against their will. But if you are going to be a Daddy, you have to be willing to do the hard things like watch the cartoons and color (lol). If you are going to be a Master, you have to do the hard things like keep the discipline. If you are a submissive, sometimes you have to kneel even when you don't feel like it. If you are a brat - what is your problem? LOL But you get my point.

This is basic shit for any relationship. If you are going to pick and choose the work you do and what you put into it, and ignore what makes the relationship work, you will end up with the equivalent of a sugar high. Your relationship will be great for a bit and then burn out quickly.

I'm writing this because I find myself guilty of this lately. Expecting the submission and babygirl stuff to be there, but what have I done to garner it? I can't choose the best parts of the dynamic and ignore the requests for attention or affirmation that our dynamic requires.

It's a dangerous spiral where the people within the relationship starve it by not nourishing it.

What a Collar Means

There are countless writings about what a collar means. And people who write more eloquently than me have described it in more flowery terms that I could ever hope to achieve. But I feel compelled to do so anyway, because I'm stubborn like that.

I came from a loveless, kinkless marriage. A marriage where my ex-wife flinched when I put on a play collar. It should have been a big clue when she had the word "obey" removed from our marriage vows. When our marriage ended, I cut up her "collar", not as a passive aggressive shitty gesture, but because it freed me more than it freed her.

Everyone does things differently. For me, collaring someone was so important to me I learned how to make both a play collar and a day collar. I'm not knocking anyone who buys them. But for me it was something that I had to build. It had to have my effort, my care, my flaws and shortcomings. Every rivet that wasn't quite flat and bit. Every link in the chain that catches on every hair. Not to sound sacrilegious, but wearing a collar is a bit like atoning for sin. The collars I make are not comfortable. Because comfortable in a relationship is the death of a relationship.

I've only every put a real collar - one I made and intended to be worn as a real collar - on one person. And that's for a good reason. I've had relationships with others. I've had strong feelings for others. But for some reason, something kept me from putting a collar on anyone else, including my ex-wife. It's because I knew they didn't value it. I couldn't trust them with it. And most importantly, they all felt temporary.

For me to put a collar on someone I have to trust them. Not just to be mine. But I have to trust them to reveal my darkest and most secret sides to them and not have them judge me or change how they look at me.

I would never put a collar on someone who didn't understand what it meant. I feel as though some submissives either don't understand the value of it or they see it as a goal to be achieved. For me, an engagement ring or wedding band has less significance. Lots of people who don't love each other or trust each other go to one knee to propose. But it takes more strength and trust and connection for a submissive to take both knees and be collared.

I'd never collar someone I didn't intend on being in my life forever.

Author's Views on Punishment

There were discussions of two things that inspired this section. The first was a writing detailing an especially harsh description of a punishment of a submissive for a repeat offense. The second was a picture used as a sort of punishment.

The question is, do these punishments go too far?

That's a good question and one we should ask frequently. However, it's not our place to determine if they go too far.

I'm sure there are even some in the kink world who think punishments are silly nonsense. Why the hell punish a man or woman? We aren't children. I admit, I had a tough time with punishments at first. But I've never just laid out a bunch of punishments I wanted to do. I've always been asked to enforce my rules through discipline, including punishment.

Personally, I don't use any sort of striking as a punishment. This is because I'm a sadist and most people I've played with are masochists. As such this blurs the lines too much. It's my OPINION that punishments should not be enjoyed, unless you are just fucking around and giving a funishment.

Secondly, growing up in a house where a belt or flyswatter was an acceptable punishment kind of put me off to this. I don't believe I should ever strike in anger if I also strike out of love and devotion.

But I think the context is what we are missing, when we ask questions like were asked about the punishments I mentioned above. We either know what the offense was but it seems harsh, or we don't know what the offense was and our mind makes up some sort of story that fits our narrative of the punishment being harsh.

Can a submissive refuse a punishment? Yes, it can happen. If it's outside the agreed upon limits they ABSOLUTELY should refuse. Within the limits. That is one of those instances where all the people in the dynamic need a cool down. I can tell you if a submissive asked me to enforce a rule then refused to take the agreed upon punishment, they would be released or at the very least we would have a talk about what was going on.

That might sound harsh but it is what it is.

For me, any punishment I give should always fit the offense or the situation. But most importantly, it must fit the dynamic. What are the agreed to limits? What is the safe word? What are the limits? If the Dominant operates within the limits of the dynamic and all limits and safe words are respected, then the harshness of the punishment and it's fit can only be assessed by the people within.

My Reset Button Got Pushed Hard - Another View on Punishment

By @kristie_kim

Sometimes my insecurities are too loud. They make me question everything from myself, to my relationships, and just my inner worth. My world spirals out of control. Everything turns into a "what if" and "could have". I can't slow it down, and it even starts to spin faster.

Luckily, I have 2 amazing guys in my life who help me stay grounded. That know how to keep these voices in check and bring me back into reality.

When the love, support, kind words, kisses, and nuzzles don't work, I need something else. To be able to have a conversation without trying to play it off as "no big deal". **If I'm upset, it is a big deal.** I get afraid to be too honest.

> *What if I say something they don't want to hear?*

But that's not the way my relationships work. We rely on open and honest communication. Sometimes I need a reminder. Sometimes I need someone force the reality back in me. To tell my "princess" to knock it the fuck off.
Yesterday was one of those days.

I was texting my Dominant one of my concerns. Of course, it wasn't just a normal question. I had been spiraling out of control for weeks. My questions feel desperate and imperative that it be solved immediately. It doesn't matter if he's busy at work. It doesn't matter that it wasn't a text conversation to be had.

I think that was the realization for him that this needed to end right now. That he was going to say something that he would regret. Even after asking me to stop, I would start it back up again. The next text stated

> *"You can sit in the corner the rest of the day and think about how you're not talking to your partner in person. Then you can come over after I get off work and the only talking that will be done is by me with you over my knee and a paddle in my hand."*

....SILENCE....

I had all day to focus on what was coming. That is the worst part for me. I love play spankings so much. I love them long and hard. The spanking I had coming was not going to be one of those.

After going over to his house that night, he brought me into the garage. He kept true to his words. He pulled up a chair, grabbed one of his hand-made paddles, and had me lay across his lap. At that moment I had so much to say. I was so angry and frustrated. To be honest, I'm not sure why I was angry.

Then he started... hard and fast. Then started asking about my behavior these last few months. Telling me how he's seen this becoming more of a problem. Telling me he has done everything he can to tell me and show me how much I am loved by my 2 amazing men.

I broke down all my walls

Any feelings I was holding back came out in a long, sobbing, snotty mess of admission. My anger turned to embarrassment. Realizing how my actions have hurt those around me. How my choices have been emotionally straining on my relationships.

After my confession he stood me up, hugged me, kissed me, and told me how important I was. In his life, my husband's life, my kids life, and in my own life. He kissed my tears and petted my hair. I knew at that moment, I was better.

After that he led me back in the house and sat me on his bed. He got us snacks and we sat in a blanket fort. Every question I had was answered. Every concern was dealt with and I didn't even feel my anxiety try to come out. I was able to have a serious and needed discussion in a calm and collected manor.

He pushed my reset button

24/7

I don't know if it's this way for everyone, but when I was stuck in a kinkless world, 24/7 D/s was both my goal and my fantasy at once. I lacked any semblance of confidence in my abilities as a Dominant or as a man. But once I was out of that relationship and into a new one where 24/7 was not only a possibility, but something we both wanted and looked forward to, we jumped at the chance.

24/7 is one of the hardest things I've ever done, and yet it is one of the most rewarding. We've been 24/7 for a little over 2 and a half years now. It's taught me a lot about myself and my partner. I think it has made us better people, better lovers, and better partners. But if I said it has all been sunshine and roses, I'd be a lying bastard.

It is HARD. And as one difficult thing is solved, two more pop up. Imagine being anything ALL THE DAMN TIME to someone. We all get breaks in our life. We can find a sitter for the kids and not be a parent for a night. We can have a girls/boys night out and not be a spouse for a night. Work ends after 8 or 12 or 24 hours and you get a break.

24/7 D/s never ends.

The collar never comes off.

The Dominant doesn't get to drop that weight.

The submissive doesn't get to quit kneeling and obeying.

It's all encompassing and never goes away and the pressure at times can seem overwhelming.

Doing D/s in the bedroom or when you can is difficult. Add in kids and jobs and bills you have to pay and parents and a house to run.

You can be talking about something completely benign, and it erupt into a fight because protocol was broken. Parents come in and think they are the Dominants in the relationship because they raised us. Um no, that won't work. Its everything you expect of a wife or husband or girlfriend or boyfriend but you have to be perfect 100% of the time.

And I can hear the naysayers now. "Well 24/7 is easy for us". Yes, it can be easy if you let things drop. Or "well if it's so hard then don't do it". Running a race is hard. Life is hard. It doesn't mean we give up. We talk about the difficulty, we work through it, and we come out the other end stronger.

The way we do it is we try to find relief valves. We do things where there's no dynamic needed. We just find fun stuff where we don't have to talk or do anything but have fun. Where it becomes meditative. Riding our Harley or clearing woods for animals. But we also do projects where one of us leads and we make something or do something that helps strengthen our dynamic. Not just protocol or D/s in the bedroom. But something that shows us we can do it, and gives us that confidence again that's needed.

Some may look at us strangely or tell us we are doing it wrong, but there are just some things I won't Dom over. The dynamic is still there, the respect is still given. But I don't Dom over things where I need a partner. She asks me if friends and family can visit. I'd never say no. She asks me about stuff with her parents. I'd never stand in the way of that. We talk about kid issues, but she knows I have the final say. It doesn't mean thta she doesn't have a voice in the relationship. It means there's a way that voice is expressed.

Overall 24/7 is hard. And there are issues and fixes that we use that I probably can't put into adequate words, because it's so complex. But if things are worth doing, people will find a way. And it's worth it to us.

Unexpected Things

There are moments in relationships that make you stop in your tracks. Something happens; an illness, a lost job, an accident, the loss of a family member, or the death of a pet. An abrupt stop to the daily grind of life and love. These are the moments of truth, the proof that your dynamic is stronger than ANYTHING life can throw at your relationship.

2 days ago I fell at derby practice, and I broke my arm. I pretty much knew it was broken the moment I got up and skated off the rink. I wasn't worried about me - I worried about what this meant for Daddy. I felt awful for putting extra stress on him, and this is what I've had to deal with as a result of my injury!!

*He has gotten up 30 mins early every day to help me with my morning routine
*He helps me get dressed and kisses my forehead.
*He helps me shower, and dry off.
*He puts my hair up in pony tails for me.
*He ties my shoes
*He puts my earrings in for me.
*He opened up my little treats.
*He makes sure i take my medicine on time.
*He encourages me that my derby life is not over.
*He reminds me it's not my fault and could happen to anyone anytime.

*He gives me extra love and hugs.
*He helps with my chores.

It is in the moments that things aren't perfect that you can see how perfect a love is. Thank you so much Daddy, for everything you have done for me. I would be so lost without you my heart.

Sub Space

The first time I sent her to subspace, I was totally lost. I admit that at the time, I had no idea what subspace was. The very few and crappy times I'd done anything with pain wasn't even close to the intensity at which we did and do things. This isn't to say we play "super hard"; it's more to say I barely played before.

I had warmed her up and I was hitting her with an implement (don't remember which one - I think it was a cane).

WHACK

"ughhh"

WHACK

"ugghhh"

WHACK

[nothing]

WHACK

[nothing]

Wait a minute.

I thought I had broken her. I stopped and asked her what was wrong. She looked confused and asked me why I stopped and I told her it was because she had stopped reacting completely.

I think we went through this process for 2-3 more play sessions before she finally said, "I think that was subspace!". That's a good clue as to how mysterious subspace is and how little people know about it.

I don't know what works for everyone. But what works for me and my sub is a rhythmic hitting. A hitting that works in a pattern at the same speed and intensity and force. The biggest sign is that all noises stop. It's like a hypnotic trance.

BUT there's also a mental component to it. The submissive has to be relaxed. But also serious mindfucks can help the pain push the submissive into subspace a little easier.

My theory is that this is some leftover primal thing from way back when. When a human wandered into a bigger predator's territory, they got that flight or fight response. But I think that oversimplifies it. I think there is also a freeze response. This is what I think subspace is. It's an overwhelmingness of pain or fear. When the bear defended its cubs by batting a human around, the best response in lieu of fight or flight was to freeze and play dead.

If you've been in nature and dealt with any prey animal, you see this. For instance, if you startle a rabbit it will run a short distance and freeze. It will freeze so bad you can almost walk all the way up on it.

It prepares prey for being hurt. This is also why the body floods the brain with endorphins and all other sorts of chemicals. It blocks out the pain so it can be endured. And floods the body with adrenaline so when the pain is over, fight or flight can take effect.

This is why I believe drop is much worse for submissives who have been into subspace. The effects on brain chemicals are just more pronounced.

Although I enjoy pushing my submissive into subspace, that is rarely the goal. Just a happy side effect.

Dom Drop

I thought this myth had gone away. But it pops up every so often.

There is a myth that Doms can't drop. We are big ole oak trees. Hard and unyielding and imposing. But that's the myth. And Doms probably don't like to admit it, but we drop. Sometimes bad.

And one can put on airs and act like they are unshakeable, but brain chemicals don't give a shit if you are 7 foot and 300 pounds. Brain chemicals don't care if you get shot at for a living or work in an office. We can't really change the way they affect us.

Dom drop happens for me when I get what I guess can be described as Dom Space. I never called it that. It's like "buck fever". For anyone who has never hunted, when you are 13 and you sit in a deer stand for the first time and a huge buck deer comes trotting up, you shake like a leaf.

That's the brain chemicals. Primarily adrenaline. There's no shame. In fact that's the primal hunter in you flooding your body with the chemicals needed to push your body to perform. When you are running across a plain, that's awesome. Trying to hold a weapon or pass rope through a knot or use a flogger - not so great.

But that adrenaline floods your body and tells it to do all sorts of things. And when that adrenaline goes away and other things replace it, there's a huge withdrawal.

I can't say what always happens during Dom Drop because I'm sure it's different for everyone. All I know is I would like to be laid on by my submissive. Not put in bondage - just to feel weight on me.

If I don't get that kind of contact, I will become very pissy. So distance between my submissive and I usually ends up in both of us dropping and fighting.

To me, avoiding drop is a team effort for both people. That can't be done if either of them are denying the effects.

Sub Drop

It might be easy as a Dominant to say that sub drop doesn't affect us. Directly it does not. However, it affects our submissives. Therefore it affects US.

I am lucky that the heaviest play I do is with my live-in partner. But when we play with others, we are still responsible for them.

My personal rules regarding play/aftercare/sub drop:

*If I or we cannot provide aftercare, we don't play.
*If I or we cannot be in touch with a play partner afterward to help them deal with sub drop, we don't play.
*If our play partner knows how they drop, we pay attention to what they say.

It's true, not everyone drops. Not everyone can recognize sub drop when it happens to them or their play partner/submissive.

So I feel it's important as the more experienced person in the dynamic to let them know what to look out for. I don't know if it's miscommunication or inexperience. But this is not happening. I get a lot of questions from submissives that just played recently (with other people) and are going through some shit they have no idea about.

*Feelings of insecurity
*Depression
*Fear
*Anxiety
*Hours or even days after

They may seem like the neediest thing in the world. But we have to embrace that and make them feel better. They suffered for us to do what we do, and although they enjoyed it, they will definitely feel the effects. It's like withdrawal from a drug. In essence, a lot of the same brain receptors are at work starving, for the chemicals that it got just a short time ago.

*Listen to their previous experiences with drop.
*Check on them often and make yourself available. The scene didn't end when the floggers and whips

got put away.
*Don't fight them or take the emotional bait.
*Help them deal with reassurance. Have them turn on their favorite music or show. Exercise also helps! And this is one time when them eating a whole pint of ice cream may be an ok way to deal.

There are some great comments below about how to deal with drop. FYI

Fun Stuff

Bondage With A little

Stuff that happens when you put a little in rope bondage...

Me: {Concentrating on something really complicated.}

her: "Pfffffffftttttt pffffftttttt. I got a hair in my mouth."

---

her: {Looking down at the rope as I tie.} "Ohhhhhhh that's pretty".

WHACK

her: "Ouchies!!!! You hit me right in the face!"

Me: "Told you to keep your eyes up!"

---

her: "Daddy do unicorns have wings?"

Me: "Nope that's a pegasus. Hold still so I can tie."

her: "What's a pegasus with a horn?"

Me: "I don't know. Shit I just lost rope ends!"

Me: "Stop wriggling!"

her: "You've got glitter in your beard. teehehee."

her (talking to another girl): The purple rope is mine. It's mine. No one else can be tied with it. Ok? Ok? OK?!"

Me: {Just finished tying and admiring it.}

her: "Daddy my foot itches."

Me: {Scratching}

her: "The other one."

Me: {Scratching} "Better?"

her: "Now the other one again..."

---

her: {Completely tied.}

Me: {Looking for sadism tools.}

her: {giggles}

Me: "What?"

her: "Why does Goofy wear clothes and Pluto doesn't? They are both dogs!"

---

her: {Breaks out in song mid-tie}

Me: "Ok, that's not distracting at all."

More Rope - A Fable

Once upon a time, a play session began.

He tied a chest harness around her delicate body; tight like a hug. The rope was beautiful on her alabaster skin.

He reached for his whip...

"More rope please, Daddy?" he heard.

So he drug out more rope and corseted her midsection all the way down. She smiled mightily.

He reached for his whip...

"More rope!" the babymonster exclaimed.

He exhausted his hemp supply tying her hands down to the bed so he moved to jute and tied her legs tight - ankles to thighs - then to the bed too.

"MORE ROPE!" the greedy babygirl demanded.

With his last hank of rope he carefully knotted up a ball gag and placed it in her mouth and around her head. Her lips stretched around it like a child trying to eat a gumball that was way too large.

Satisfied, he reached again for his whip...

"ORRRE OPPPPPPE" she muttered around the gag.

He got the old boat rope from the shed. He got the old climbing rope from off the tree outside. He took down the clotheslines. He brought it all in and tied and tied and tied until she looked like a fly caught by a spider. Nothing but a head peeking out.

He carefully reached for the whip while keeping an eye on her (but he knew not what was left to whip).

"oorrre ooooopppe" she said once again.

He took her gag out.

"More rope, more rope more rope" she said while somehow bouncing though all the ties.

He stuck his cock deep into her throat in a last ditch effort to shut her up. He thrusted and thrusted. Drool and spittle and precum spilled out the sides of her mouth while she sung.

"mooorrrrreeeee roooooooppppppeeeee"

So he withdrew and shot ropes across her face.

"Tankies Daddyyyyyy" she finally said.

Erotica For littles

As I swung the front door open, she was standing there wearing nothing but pigtails and an evil grin. She slowly drew a lollipop out of her mouth.

"Daddy has something you can put in your mouth," I said as I reached into my pants and pulled out...

TWO MORE LOLLIPOPS!

She bounced so hard she nearly hit the ceiling and took the lollipops from me.

"Now for the real surprise!" I said as I pulled a pack of gummies out of another pocket.

SQUEEEEEEEEEEEEEEEEE.

Then we watched cartoons and cuddled until bedtime.

Then it was on as we had raunchy raunchy group sex with three friends. Bear bear - who is an older dude. He's missing an eye but that makes him tough. And muffin - she's long and lean and young. And Dory - she forgets a lot but she's eager.

Then when I was done with her I gave her the real surprise. Something she could suck on.

More Lollipops!!!

Performing Oral On a Bratty babygirl

*You get glitter in your beard and are henceforth known as Captain Glitterbeard.

*She will later change your name in her phone to Captain Glitterbeard and realize that there are too many letters. And then laugh when it reads "Captain Glitterbear".

*When she lays back on the bed her right leg will shake like a dog wagging its tail.

*She will put her cold ass feet on your back and laugh about it.

*She will call you all sorts of names for making her cum too quickly. "You asshole, too quick!!"

*When you slow down she will ask why you slowed down.

*She will try to grab your head but her little T-rex arms will never reach.

*She will use a stuffy to compensate for her T-rex arms so she can reach you.

*When her toes curl she will grip your back skin with her toes. It hurts but its what I get for not stopping once she cums.

Daddy Please...

Sit on the floor and color pictures with me while we watch silly movies. I'm sorry I spilled glitter everywhere, I just wanted it to be sparkly and pretty. I tried my best to clean it up all by myself. Aren't you proud of me?

Giggles, I'm sorry Daddy; I know there are too many stuffies on the bed. How about I move my pony, Dory, and toothless so you can fit in the bed better. I know they drive you crazy, but tankies for buying them all for me. I love them all so much.

Pull me into your arms and squeeze me tight. I had a bad day and you're the only thing that will make me feel happy again. I'm sorry I'm needy and emotional today. Thank you for holding me extra long and tight. My forehead kissies helped the mostest.

Daaaaadddyyy I'm hungry. Can you please make me "ants on a log?" I can't make them as good as you do. Your peanut butter to raisin ratio is far superior. Taaankies Daddy they are super nummy.

Please Daddy... I'm so overwhelmed by life. I can't find my center. I'm lost. Hurt me Daddy. Remind me that my place in this world is kneeling safely at your feet. Only to be used by you. Put all my fractured pieces back together one amazing orgasm at a time.

Daddy, I can't sleep. Will you read me a story and pet me till I fall asleep? I promise I won't wiggle the rest of the night. Thank you for not getting frustrated when I beg for one more because the sound of your voice is more addictive then heroin.

I didn't mean to wake you up Daddy. The thunder was really loud, and Bear Bear got scared. Not me though, I'm brave.... but can we snuggle up closer to you anyway? For Bear Bear?

I'm sorry I text you a hundred times a day. I just miss you so much when we are apart. Thank you for never making me feel needy, and paying me extra attentions.

I know the weight of the world is on your shoulders Daddy, let me help carry it. I'm stronger than I look. I can helps you too. Let me kneel at your feet, use me until your stresses float away. Place my collar around my neck and let me massage every sore tired muscle you have. Please Daddy, let me take care of you too.

Fun Activities For Daddy/little

*Zoos, aquariums, planetariums and nature reserves
*Camping
*Playing at the park
*Arcades (especially those with ticket rewards)
*Coloring books
*Cooking or making treats (see next section)
*Watching cartoons or movies that appeal to them
*Painting lessons
*Roller or Ice Skating
*Making stuffies at Build-A-Bear
*Making blanket forts and playing a game.
*Going to the circus
*Crafts like those found at Hobby Lobby (we made concrete stepping stones.

Fun Treats for littles

*"ants on apples"- 1/4 apple, smother in peanut butter, sprinkle with raisins.

*fluffer-nutter sandwiches" peanut butter and marshmallow with the crusty cut off.

*"foodles" these are found at Wal-mart and are shaped like a certain famous mouse and full of treats. there is another one that is a certain group of dog superheroes.

*animal crackers with nutella

*little gerber yogurt drops.

*fruities/fruit roll ups.

*Ice cream pop

Made in the USA
Middletown, DE
25 September 2023